This book belongs to

_____

Date: _____

# HOW DID THINGS GO TODAY?

What didn't totally suck?

_____

_____

_____

_____

What was actually kind of cool?

_____

_____

_____

_____

What are you excited to do tomorrow?

_____

_____

_____

_____

Date: _____

# HOW DID THINGS GO TODAY?

What didn't totally suck?

_____
_____
_____
_____

What was actually kind of cool?

_____
_____
_____
_____

What are you excited to do tomorrow?

_____
_____
_____
_____

Date: _____

# HOW DID THINGS GO TODAY?

## What didn't totally suck?

_____

_____

_____

_____

## What was actually kind of cool?

_____

_____

_____

_____

## What are you excited to do tomorrow?

_____

_____

_____

_____

Date: _____

# HOW DID THINGS GO TODAY?

What didn't totally suck?

_____
_____
_____
_____

What was actually kind of cool?

_____
_____
_____
_____

What are you excited to do tomorrow?

_____
_____
_____
_____

Date: _____

# HOW DID THINGS GO TODAY?

What didn't totally suck?

_____

_____

_____

_____

What was actually kind of cool?

_____

_____

_____

_____

What are you excited to do tomorrow?

_____

_____

_____

_____

Date: _____

# HOW DID THINGS GO TODAY?

## What didn't totally suck?

_____
_____
_____
_____

## What was actually kind of cool?

_____
_____
_____
_____

## What are you excited to do tomorrow?

_____
_____
_____
_____

Date: _____

# HOW DID THINGS GO TODAY?

What didn't totally suck?

_____

_____

_____

_____

What was actually kind of cool?

_____

_____

_____

_____

What are you excited to do tomorrow?

_____

_____

_____

_____

Date: _____

# HOW DID THINGS GO TODAY?

### What didn't totally suck?

_____
_____
_____
_____

### What was actually kind of cool?

_____
_____
_____
_____

### What are you excited to do tomorrow?

_____
_____
_____
_____

Date: _____

# HOW DID THINGS GO TODAY?

What didn't totally suck?

_____
_____
_____
_____

What was actually kind of cool?

_____
_____
_____
_____

What are you excited to do tomorrow?

_____
_____
_____
_____

Date: _____

# HOW DID THINGS GO TODAY?

What didn't totally suck?

_____
_____
_____
_____

What was actually kind of cool?

_____
_____
_____
_____

What are you excited to do tomorrow?

_____
_____
_____
_____

Date: _____

# HOW DID THINGS GO TODAY?

What didn't totally suck?

_____

_____

_____

_____

What was actually kind of cool?

_____

_____

_____

_____

What are you excited to do tomorrow?

_____

_____

_____

_____

Date: _____

# HOW DID THINGS GO TODAY?

What didn't totally suck?

_____

_____

_____

_____

What was actually kind of cool?

_____

_____

_____

_____

What are you excited to do tomorrow?

_____

_____

_____

_____

Date: _____

# HOW DID THINGS GO TODAY?

What didn't totally suck?

_____

_____

_____

_____

What was actually kind of cool?

_____

_____

_____

_____

What are you excited to do tomorrow?

_____

_____

_____

_____

Date: _____

# HOW DID THINGS GO TODAY?

What didn't totally suck?

_____

_____

_____

_____

What was actually kind of cool?

_____

_____

_____

_____

What are you excited to do tomorrow?

_____

_____

_____

_____

Date: _____

# HOW DID THINGS GO TODAY?

What didn't totally suck?

_____

_____

_____

_____

What was actually kind of cool?

_____

_____

_____

_____

What are you excited to do tomorrow?

_____

_____

_____

_____

Date: _____

# HOW DID THINGS GO TODAY?

What didn't totally suck?

_____

_____

_____

_____

What was actually kind of cool?

_____

_____

_____

_____

What are you excited to do tomorrow?

_____

_____

_____

_____

Date: _____

# HOW DID THINGS GO TODAY?

What didn't totally suck?

_____

_____

_____

_____

What was actually kind of cool?

_____

_____

_____

_____

What are you excited to do tomorrow?

_____

_____

_____

_____

Date: _____

# HOW DID THINGS GO TODAY?

What didn't totally suck?

_____

_____

_____

_____

What was actually kind of cool?

_____

_____

_____

_____

What are you excited to do tomorrow?

_____

_____

_____

_____

Date: _____

# HOW DID THINGS GO TODAY?

What didn't totally suck?

_____

_____

_____

_____

What was actually kind of cool?

_____

_____

_____

_____

What are you excited to do tomorrow?

_____

_____

_____

_____

Date: _____

# HOW DID THINGS GO TODAY?

## What didn't totally suck?

_____

_____

_____

_____

## What was actually kind of cool?

_____

_____

_____

_____

## What are you excited to do tomorrow?

_____

_____

_____

_____

Date: _____

# HOW DID THINGS GO TODAY?

What didn't totally suck?

_____

_____

_____

_____

What was actually kind of cool?

_____

_____

_____

_____

What are you excited to do tomorrow?

_____

_____

_____

_____

Date: _____

# HOW DID THINGS GO TODAY?

What didn't totally suck?

_____

_____

_____

_____

What was actually kind of cool?

_____

_____

_____

_____

What are you excited to do tomorrow?

_____

_____

_____

_____

Date: _____

# HOW DID THINGS GO TODAY?

## What didn't totally suck?

_____
_____
_____
_____

## What was actually kind of cool?

_____
_____
_____
_____

## What are you excited to do tomorrow?

_____
_____
_____
_____

Date: _____

# HOW DID THINGS GO TODAY?

What didn't totally suck?

_____

_____

_____

_____

What was actually kind of cool?

_____

_____

_____

_____

What are you excited to do tomorrow?

_____

_____

_____

_____

Date: _____

# HOW DID THINGS GO TODAY?

What didn't totally suck?

_____

_____

_____

_____

What was actually kind of cool?

_____

_____

_____

_____

What are you excited to do tomorrow?

_____

_____

_____

_____

Date: _____

# HOW DID THINGS GO TODAY?

What didn't totally suck?

_____
_____
_____
_____

What was actually kind of cool?

_____
_____
_____
_____

What are you excited to do tomorrow?

_____
_____
_____
_____

Date: _____

# HOW DID THINGS GO TODAY?

What didn't totally suck?

_____
_____
_____
_____

What was actually kind of cool?

_____
_____
_____
_____

What are you excited to do tomorrow?

_____
_____
_____
_____

Date: _____

# HOW DID THINGS GO TODAY?

What didn't totally suck?

_____
_____
_____
_____

What was actually kind of cool?

_____
_____
_____
_____

What are you excited to do tomorrow?

_____
_____
_____
_____

Date: _____

# HOW DID THINGS GO TODAY?

What didn't totally suck?

_____

_____

_____

_____

What was actually kind of cool?

_____

_____

_____

_____

What are you excited to do tomorrow?

_____

_____

_____

_____

Date: _____

# HOW DID THINGS GO TODAY?

What didn't totally suck?

_____

_____

_____

_____

What was actually kind of cool?

_____

_____

_____

_____

What are you excited to do tomorrow?

_____

_____

_____

_____

Date: _____

# HOW DID THINGS GO TODAY?

What didn't totally suck?

_____

_____

_____

_____

What was actually kind of cool?

_____

_____

_____

_____

What are you excited to do tomorrow?

_____

_____

_____

_____

Date: _____

# HOW DID THINGS GO TODAY?

What didn't totally suck?

_____
_____
_____
_____

What was actually kind of cool?

_____
_____
_____
_____

What are you excited to do tomorrow?

_____
_____
_____
_____

Date: _____

# HOW DID THINGS GO TODAY?

What didn't totally suck?

_____
_____
_____
_____

What was actually kind of cool?

_____
_____
_____
_____

What are you excited to do tomorrow?

_____
_____
_____
_____

Date: _____

# HOW DID THINGS GO TODAY?

What didn't totally suck?

_____
_____
_____
_____

What was actually kind of cool?

_____
_____
_____
_____

What are you excited to do tomorrow?

_____
_____
_____
_____

Date: _____

# HOW DID THINGS GO TODAY?

What didn't totally suck?

_____

_____

_____

_____

What was actually kind of cool?

_____

_____

_____

_____

What are you excited to do tomorrow?

_____

_____

_____

_____

Date: _____

# HOW DID THINGS GO TODAY?

What didn't totally suck?

_____

_____

_____

_____

What was actually kind of cool?

_____

_____

_____

_____

What are you excited to do tomorrow?

_____

_____

_____

_____

Date: _____

# HOW DID THINGS GO TODAY?

What didn't totally suck?

_____
_____
_____
_____

What was actually kind of cool?

_____
_____
_____
_____

What are you excited to do tomorrow?

_____
_____
_____
_____

Date: _____

# HOW DID THINGS GO TODAY?

What didn't totally suck?

_____
_____
_____
_____

What was actually kind of cool?

_____
_____
_____
_____

What are you excited to do tomorrow?

_____
_____
_____
_____

Date: _____

# HOW DID THINGS GO TODAY?

### What didn't totally suck?

_____

_____

_____

_____

### What was actually kind of cool?

_____

_____

_____

_____

### What are you excited to do tomorrow?

_____

_____

_____

_____

Date: _____

# HOW DID THINGS GO TODAY?

What didn't totally suck?

_____

_____

_____

_____

What was actually kind of cool?

_____

_____

_____

_____

What are you excited to do tomorrow?

_____

_____

_____

_____

Date: _____

# HOW DID THINGS GO TODAY?

What didn't totally suck?

_____

_____

_____

_____

What was actually kind of cool?

_____

_____

_____

What are you excited to do tomorrow?

_____

_____

_____

_____

Date: _____

# HOW DID THINGS GO TODAY?

## What didn't totally suck?

_____

_____

_____

_____

## What was actually kind of cool?

_____

_____

_____

_____

## What are you excited to do tomorrow?

_____

_____

_____

_____

Date: _____

# HOW DID THINGS GO TODAY?

What didn't totally suck?

_____

_____

_____

_____

What was actually kind of cool?

_____

_____

_____

_____

What are you excited to do tomorrow?

_____

_____

_____

_____

Date: _____

# HOW DID THINGS GO TODAY?

What didn't totally suck?

_____
_____
_____
_____

What was actually kind of cool?

_____
_____
_____
_____

What are you excited to do tomorrow?

_____
_____
_____
_____

Date: _____

# HOW DID THINGS GO TODAY?

What didn't totally suck?

_____

_____

_____

_____

What was actually kind of cool?

_____

_____

_____

What are you excited to do tomorrow?

_____

_____

_____

Date: _____

# HOW DID THINGS GO TODAY?

## What didn't totally suck?

_____

_____

_____

_____

## What was actually kind of cool?

_____

_____

_____

_____

## What are you excited to do tomorrow?

_____

_____

_____

_____

Date: _____

# HOW DID THINGS GO TODAY?

What didn't totally suck?

_____

_____

_____

_____

What was actually kind of cool?

_____

_____

_____

_____

What are you excited to do tomorrow?

_____

_____

_____

_____

Date: _____

# HOW DID THINGS GO TODAY?

### What didn't totally suck?

_____
_____
_____
_____

### What was actually kind of cool?

_____
_____
_____
_____

### What are you excited to do tomorrow?

_____
_____
_____
_____

Date: _____

# HOW DID THINGS GO TODAY?

What didn't totally suck?

_____

_____

_____

_____

What was actually kind of cool?

_____

_____

_____

_____

What are you excited to do tomorrow?

_____

_____

_____

_____

Date: _____

# HOW DID THINGS GO TODAY?

What didn't totally suck?

_____
_____
_____
_____

What was actually kind of cool?

_____
_____
_____
_____

What are you excited to do tomorrow?

_____
_____
_____
_____

Date: _____

# HOW DID THINGS GO TODAY?

What didn't totally suck?

_____
_____
_____
_____

What was actually kind of cool?

_____
_____
_____

What are you excited to do tomorrow?

_____
_____
_____
_____

Date: _____

# HOW DID THINGS GO TODAY?

What didn't totally suck?

_____

_____

_____

_____

What was actually kind of cool?

_____

_____

_____

_____

What are you excited to do tomorrow?

_____

_____

_____

_____

Date: _____

# HOW DID THINGS GO TODAY?

What didn't totally suck?

_____
_____
_____
_____

What was actually kind of cool?

_____
_____
_____
_____

What are you excited to do tomorrow?

_____
_____
_____
_____

Date: _____

# HOW DID THINGS GO TODAY?

### What didn't totally suck?

_____

_____

_____

_____

### What was actually kind of cool?

_____

_____

_____

_____

### What are you excited to do tomorrow?

_____

_____

_____

_____

Date: _____

# HOW DID THINGS GO TODAY?

What didn't totally suck?

_____

_____

_____

_____

What was actually kind of cool?

_____

_____

_____

_____

What are you excited to do tomorrow?

_____

_____

_____

_____

Date: _____

# HOW DID THINGS GO TODAY?

What didn't totally suck?

_____
_____
_____
_____

What was actually kind of cool?

_____
_____
_____
_____

What are you excited to do tomorrow?

_____
_____
_____
_____

Date: _____

# HOW DID THINGS GO TODAY?

### What didn't totally suck?

_____

_____

_____

_____

### What was actually kind of cool?

_____

_____

_____

_____

### What are you excited to do tomorrow?

_____

_____

_____

_____

Date: _____

# HOW DID THINGS GO TODAY?

What didn't totally suck?

_____

_____

_____

_____

What was actually kind of cool?

_____

_____

_____

_____

What are you excited to do tomorrow?

_____

_____

_____

_____

Date: _____

# HOW DID THINGS GO TODAY?

What didn't totally suck?

_____

_____

_____

_____

What was actually kind of cool?

_____

_____

_____

_____

What are you excited to do tomorrow?

_____

_____

_____

_____

Date: _____

# HOW DID THINGS GO TODAY?

What didn't totally suck?

_____

_____

_____

_____

What was actually kind of cool?

_____

_____

_____

_____

What are you excited to do tomorrow?

_____

_____

_____

_____

Date: _____

# HOW DID THINGS GO TODAY?

What didn't totally suck?

_____
_____
_____
_____

What was actually kind of cool?

_____
_____
_____
_____

What are you excited to do tomorrow?

_____
_____
_____
_____

Date: _____

# HOW DID THINGS GO TODAY?

### What didn't totally suck?

_____

_____

_____

_____

### What was actually kind of cool?

_____

_____

_____

_____

### What are you excited to do tomorrow?

_____

_____

_____

_____

Date: _____

# HOW DID THINGS GO TODAY?

What didn't totally suck?

_____

_____

_____

_____

What was actually kind of cool?

_____

_____

_____

_____

What are you excited to do tomorrow?

_____

_____

_____

_____

Date: _____

# HOW DID THINGS GO TODAY?

What didn't totally suck?

_____

_____

_____

_____

What was actually kind of cool?

_____

_____

_____

_____

What are you excited to do tomorrow?

_____

_____

_____

_____

Date: _____

# HOW DID THINGS GO TODAY?

What didn't totally suck?

_____

_____

_____

_____

What was actually kind of cool?

_____

_____

_____

_____

What are you excited to do tomorrow?

_____

_____

_____

_____

Date: _____

# HOW DID THINGS GO TODAY?

What didn't totally suck?

_____

_____

_____

_____

What was actually kind of cool?

_____

_____

_____

What are you excited to do tomorrow?

_____

_____

_____

_____

Date: _____

# HOW DID THINGS GO TODAY?

What didn't totally suck?

_____

_____

_____

_____

What was actually kind of cool?

_____

_____

_____

_____

What are you excited to do tomorrow?

_____

_____

_____

_____

Date: _____

# HOW DID THINGS GO TODAY?

### What didn't totally suck?

_____

_____

_____

_____

### What was actually kind of cool?

_____

_____

_____

_____

### What are you excited to do tomorrow?

_____

_____

_____

_____

Date: _____

# HOW DID THINGS GO TODAY?

What didn't totally suck?

_____

_____

_____

_____

What was actually kind of cool?

_____

_____

_____

_____

What are you excited to do tomorrow?

_____

_____

_____

_____

Date: _____

# HOW DID THINGS GO TODAY?

What didn't totally suck?

_____

_____

_____

_____

What was actually kind of cool?

_____

_____

_____

_____

What are you excited to do tomorrow?

_____

_____

_____

_____

Date: _____

# HOW DID THINGS GO TODAY?

What didn't totally suck?

_____

_____

_____

_____

What was actually kind of cool?

_____

_____

_____

_____

What are you excited to do tomorrow?

_____

_____

_____

_____

Date: _____

# HOW DID THINGS GO TODAY?

What didn't totally suck?

_____

_____

_____

_____

What was actually kind of cool?

_____

_____

_____

_____

What are you excited to do tomorrow?

_____

_____

_____

_____

Date: _____

# HOW DID THINGS GO TODAY?

What didn't totally suck?

_____

_____

_____

_____

What was actually kind of cool?

_____

_____

_____

_____

What are you excited to do tomorrow?

_____

_____

_____

_____

Date: _____

# HOW DID THINGS GO TODAY?

What didn't totally suck?

_____
_____
_____
_____

What was actually kind of cool?

_____
_____
_____
_____

What are you excited to do tomorrow?

_____
_____
_____
_____

Date: _____

# HOW DID THINGS GO TODAY?

What didn't totally suck?

_____
_____
_____
_____

What was actually kind of cool?

_____
_____
_____
_____

What are you excited to do tomorrow?

_____
_____
_____
_____

Date: _____

# HOW DID THINGS GO TODAY?

What didn't totally suck?

_____

_____

_____

_____

What was actually kind of cool?

_____

_____

_____

_____

What are you excited to do tomorrow?

_____

_____

_____

_____

Date: _____

# HOW DID THINGS GO TODAY?

What didn't totally suck?

_____

_____

_____

_____

What was actually kind of cool?

_____

_____

_____

_____

What are you excited to do tomorrow?

_____

_____

_____

_____

Date: _____

# HOW DID THINGS GO TODAY?

### What didn't totally suck?

_____

_____

_____

_____

### What was actually kind of cool?

_____

_____

_____

_____

### What are you excited to do tomorrow?

_____

_____

_____

_____

Date: _____

# HOW DID THINGS GO TODAY?

What didn't totally suck?

_____

_____

_____

_____

What was actually kind of cool?

_____

_____

_____

What are you excited to do tomorrow?

_____

_____

_____

Date: _____

# HOW DID THINGS GO TODAY?

What didn't totally suck?

_____
_____
_____
_____

What was actually kind of cool?

_____
_____
_____
_____

What are you excited to do tomorrow?

_____
_____
_____
_____

Date: _____

# HOW DID THINGS GO TODAY?

What didn't totally suck?

_____

_____

_____

_____

What was actually kind of cool?

_____

_____

_____

_____

What are you excited to do tomorrow?

_____

_____

_____

_____

Date: _____

# HOW DID THINGS GO TODAY?

What didn't totally suck?

_____
_____
_____
_____

What was actually kind of cool?

_____
_____
_____
_____

What are you excited to do tomorrow?

_____
_____
_____
_____

Date: _____

# HOW DID THINGS GO TODAY?

What didn't totally suck?

_____

_____

_____

_____

What was actually kind of cool?

_____

_____

_____

_____

What are you excited to do tomorrow?

_____

_____

_____

_____

Date: _____

# HOW DID THINGS GO TODAY?

What didn't totally suck?

_____
_____
_____
_____

What was actually kind of cool?

_____
_____
_____
_____

What are you excited to do tomorrow?

_____
_____
_____
_____

Date: _____

# HOW DID THINGS GO TODAY?

What didn't totally suck?

_____

_____

_____

_____

What was actually kind of cool?

_____

_____

_____

_____

What are you excited to do tomorrow?

_____

_____

_____

_____

Date: _____

# HOW DID THINGS GO TODAY?

What didn't totally suck?

_____
_____
_____
_____

What was actually kind of cool?

_____
_____
_____
_____

What are you excited to do tomorrow?

_____
_____
_____
_____

Date: _____

# HOW DID THINGS GO TODAY?

What didn't totally suck?

_____

_____

_____

_____

What was actually kind of cool?

_____

_____

_____

_____

What are you excited to do tomorrow?

_____

_____

_____

_____

Date: _____

# HOW DID THINGS GO TODAY?

What didn't totally suck?

_____

_____

_____

_____

What was actually kind of cool?

_____

_____

_____

_____

What are you excited to do tomorrow?

_____

_____

_____

_____

Date: _____

# HOW DID THINGS GO TODAY?

What didn't totally suck?

_____

_____

_____

_____

What was actually kind of cool?

_____

_____

_____

_____

What are you excited to do tomorrow?

_____

_____

_____

_____

Date: _____

# HOW DID THINGS GO TODAY?

### What didn't totally suck?

_____

_____

_____

_____

### What was actually kind of cool?

_____

_____

_____

_____

### What are you excited to do tomorrow?

_____

_____

_____

_____

Date: _____

# HOW DID THINGS GO TODAY?

What didn't totally suck?

_____

_____

_____

_____

What was actually kind of cool?

_____

_____

_____

_____

What are you excited to do tomorrow?

_____

_____

_____

_____

Date: _____

# HOW DID THINGS GO TODAY?

What didn't totally suck?

_____

_____

_____

_____

What was actually kind of cool?

_____

_____

_____

_____

What are you excited to do tomorrow?

_____

_____

_____

_____

Date: _____

# HOW DID THINGS GO TODAY?

## What didn't totally suck?

_____

_____

_____

_____

## What was actually kind of cool?

_____

_____

_____

_____

## What are you excited to do tomorrow?

_____

_____

_____

_____

Date: _____

# HOW DID THINGS GO TODAY?

What didn't totally suck?

_____

_____

_____

_____

What was actually kind of cool?

_____

_____

_____

_____

What are you excited to do tomorrow?

_____

_____

_____

_____

Date: _____

# HOW DID THINGS GO TODAY?

What didn't totally suck?

_____
_____
_____
_____

What was actually kind of cool?

_____
_____
_____
_____

What are you excited to do tomorrow?

_____
_____
_____
_____

Date: _____

# HOW DID THINGS GO TODAY?

What didn't totally suck?

_____

_____

_____

_____

What was actually kind of cool?

_____

_____

_____

_____

What are you excited to do tomorrow?

_____

_____

_____

_____

Date: _____

# HOW DID THINGS GO TODAY?

### What didn't totally suck?

_____

_____

_____

_____

### What was actually kind of cool?

_____

_____

_____

_____

### What are you excited to do tomorrow?

_____

_____

_____

_____

Date: _____

# HOW DID THINGS GO TODAY?

What didn't totally suck?

_____
_____
_____
_____

What was actually kind of cool?

_____
_____
_____
_____

What are you excited to do tomorrow?

_____
_____
_____
_____

Date: _____

# HOW DID THINGS GO TODAY?

What didn't totally suck?

_____

_____

_____

What was actually kind of cool?

_____

_____

_____

What are you excited to do tomorrow?

_____

_____

_____

Date: _____

# HOW DID THINGS GO TODAY?

What didn't totally suck?

_____

_____

_____

_____

What was actually kind of cool?

_____

_____

_____

_____

What are you excited to do tomorrow?

_____

_____

_____

_____

Made in the USA
Coppell, TX
25 January 2022